Greater Than a .... Series
Reviews from Readers

Great ideas for a port day.

-Mary Martin USA

Aptly titled, you won't just be a tourist after reading this book. You'll be greater than a tourist!

-Alan Warner, Grand Rapids, USA

Even though I only have three days to spend in San Miguel in an upcoming visit, I will use the author's suggestions to guide some of my time there. An easy read - with chapters named to guide me in directions I want to go.

 -Robert Catapano, USA

Great insights from a local perspective! Useful information and a very good value!

 -Sarah, USA

This series provides an in-depth experience through the eyes of a local. Reading these series will help you to travel the city in with confidence and it'll make your journey a unique one.

-Andrew Teoh, Ipoh, Malaysia

GREATER THAN A TOURIST- ST. GALLEN SWITZERLAND

50 Travel Tips from a Local

Isabelle Howells

Cover designed by: Ivana Stamenkovic
Cover Image: https://pixabay.com/photos/st-gallen-historic-center-2868022/

CZYK Publishing Since 2011.

Greater Than a Tourist

Lock Haven, PA
All rights reserved.

ISBN: 9781692759728

>TOURIST

50 TRAVEL TIPS FROM A LOCAL

BOOK DESCRIPTION

Are you excited about planning your next trip? Do you want to try something new? Would you like some guidance from a local? If you answered yes to any of these questions, then this Greater Than a Tourist book is for you. *Greater Than a Tourist – St. Gallen, Switzerland* by Isabelle Howells offers the inside scoop on St. Gallen. Most travel books tell you how to travel like a tourist. Although there is nothing wrong with that, as part of the Greater Than a Tourist series, this book will give you travel tips from someone who has lived at your next travel destination.

In these pages, you will discover advice that will help you throughout your stay. This book will not tell you exact addresses or store hours but instead will give you excitement and knowledge from a local that you may not find in other smaller print travel books.

Travel like a local. Slow down, stay in one place, and get to know the people and culture. By the time you finish this book, you will be eager and prepared to travel to your next destination.

Inside this travel guide book you will find:

- Insider tips from a local.

- Packing and planning list.

- List of travel questions to ask yourself or others while traveling.

- A place to write your travel bucket list.

OUR STORY

Traveling is a passion of the Greater than a Tourist book series creator. Lisa studied abroad in college, and for their honeymoon Lisa and her husband toured Europe. During her travels to Malta, an older man tried to give her some advice based on his own experience living on the island since he was a young boy. She was not sure if she should talk to the stranger but was interested in his advice. When traveling to some places she was wary to talk to locals because she was afraid that they weren't being genuine. Through her travels, Lisa learned how much locals had to share with tourists. Lisa created the Greater Than a Tourist book series to help connect people with locals. A topic that locals are very passionate about sharing.

TABLE OF CONTENTS

NOTES

DEDICATION

This book is dedicated to all of my travel partners, past, present (and future), who have helped me explore the world and myself.

ABOUT THE AUTHOR

Isabelle Howells is British but now lives in Zurich, Switzerland. She moved there more than ten years ago, when her job brought her to the Land of Milk and Money. During this time, she has become obsessed with exploring the beautiful country that she now calls home and spends her time uncovering hidden gems in the Swiss countryside.

She loves to travel all over the world, especially if it means discovering new cultures and new foods. When she is not travelling, she enjoys cooking, reading and drinking good wine.

Isabelle is always happy to share travel tips with her fellow explorers.

HOW TO USE THIS BOOK

The *Greater Than a Tourist* book series was written by someone who has lived in an area for over three months. The goal of this book is to help travelers either dream or experience different locations by providing opinions from a local. The author has made suggestions based on their own experiences. Please check before traveling to the area in case the suggested places are unavailable.

Travel Advisories: As a first step in planning any trip abroad, check the Travel Advisories for your intended destination.
https://travel.state.gov/content/travel/en/traveladvisories/traveladvisories.html

FROM THE PUBLISHER

Traveling can be one of the most important parts of a person's life. The anticipation and memories that you have are some of the best. As a publisher of the Greater Than a Tourist, as well as the popular *50 Things to Know* book series, we strive to help you learn about new places, spark your imagination, and inspire you. Wherever you are and whatever you do I wish you safe, fun, and inspiring travel.

Lisa Rusczyk Ed. D.
CZYK Publishing

WELCOME TO
> TOURIST

"Travel makes one modest. You see what a tiny place you occupy in the world."

- Gustav Flaubert

St Gallen
Switzerland

St. Gallen Climate

	High	Low
January	36	27
February	38	28
March	46	34
April	53	39
May	61	47
June	67	53
July	71	56
August	70	56
September	62	50
October	54	43
November	44	34
December	39	29

GreaterThanaTourist.com

Temperatures are in Fahrenheit degrees.
Source: NOAA

THE BASICS

1. WHY VISIT?

Located in Eastern Switzerland, St Gallen is blessed with being surrounded by the beauty of the Alps, an area that has been listed as a UNESCO World Heritage Site. It is a hidden gem in the Swiss landscape. Often it is overlooked as a travel destination, with people favouring more well-known places to spend their time while on holiday in Switzerland.

People who miss visiting St Gallen are really missing out. The small Swiss town is home to some of the world's most famous cheese, chocolate and beer producers, has amazing views of the Alps and is a place steeped in tradition.

It also marries together the traditions of the old and more modern, adventurous past times. You can enjoy nature, hiking or other leisure sports or wander through the historic Old Town, which is closed to traffic.

A trip to St Gallen is definitely worth it! And with these tips you will be able to enjoy this charming place with something to keep all of the family entertaining during your stay.

2. USEFUL PHRASES

St Gallen is located in the German-speaking part of Switzerland. Although German is one of the four official languages in the country, you will hear the locals speak to each other in a dialect form of German. The dialect differs from canton to canton, so much so that the Swiss sometimes find it difficult to understand their fellow countrymen, despite living a few kilometres away from each other

However, the most common words and phrases remain the same throughout the German-speaking cantons.

Here are a handful of words that you might hear in everyday situations and might find useful:

Grüzei – Good morning (formal)

Hoi – Good morning (informal)

En Guete – Bon Appetit

Prost! – Cheers

3. CURRENCY TO CARRY

The currency in Switzerland is the Swiss Franc (CHF). It is also accepted in the small principality of Liechtenstein, which is less than an hour's drive by car from St. Gallen.

You can exchange money at all airports and large train stations in Switzerland. Check before you exchange if there are any hidden fees or commissions.

Don't worry if you don't have the correct change. Although wireless card payments are becoming more and more common, Swiss people still rely heavily on cash to pay for goods. It is possible to pay for small items with large bank notes. Everyone always has change, so don't feel embarrassed if you don't have anything smaller. Even isolated restaurants on top of mountains will be able to break a 100 CHF note.

4. HOW TO GET AROUND

The best way to get around is using public transport. All of the things you have heard about the transport system in Switzerland are true: it's reliable, clean and good for the environment.

But there has to be at least one drawback: as a tourist, it can be an expensive way to travel.

If you are staying in Switzerland for extended period of time with the intention of utilizing public transport, it is best to invest in a travel card that gives you unlimited access to all rail, road and waterways throughout Switzerland.

Options include travel with a Half-Tax card, which is valid for one month, that will entitle you to half price travel throughout the whole Swiss network, or a Day Pass for either 3, 4, 8 or 15 days for unlimited travel.

You can find all the details on the SBB website.

Beware: travelling without a valid ticket is a very expensive business and you would be best to avoid. If your ticket is not valid you face a minimum fine of 100 CHF plus the cost of a valid ticket for the journey that you are making. Ticket inspectors will also take your details to keep on file and repeat offenders will be fined more heavily.

5. APPS TO DOWNLOAD BEFORE YOU ARRIVE

If you are going to be taking advantage of the excellent public transport system, I highly recommend downloading the SBB app. The app is very easy to use and gives you up to date information about the latest arrivals and departures for all modes of transport. Connections as well as the platform information is also clearly displayed.

The best app for weather is MeteoSwiss. The app tends to give more accurate information about the hourly weather than other apps that might already be installed on your phone.

If you want to keep a grip on your finances make sure that you download the XE currency app. You can select your home currency and up to 10 other currency to convert prices quickly and easily, so this is handy for anywhere you travel.

However, I would advise caution at looking up the prices of everything that you intend to buy. Prices are in Switzerland are known for being more expensive than most of the rest of the world and, if you look up the equivalent price in your home currency, you might be both a little shocked and reluctant to flash the cash. You might only visit Switzerland once in your lifetime so make the most of it.

You can always earn more money, but memories can only be made once!

6. STAY SAFE

Switzerland has a very low crime rate and is an extremely safe place to travel by yourself. It's also perfectly safe to walk around by yourself at night.

However, everywhere that attracts tourists, also attracts people who are looking to take advantage of others. I have heard of bags being taken in very busy tourist spots, such as popular restaurants, without the owner even realising until she came to pay for her meal. So please be as vigilant as you would be anywhere else in the world. The quaint streets and cities can easily lull you into a false sense of security but you should still be alert to the potential dangers of theft.

Additionally, if you are intending to go hiking and enjoy more of the stunning scenery from a different view point, make sure that you are properly equipped. Check the weather before you set off so that you can take the right clothes with you and make sure that you have enough water and refreshments for the whole trip.

7. WHO TO ASK FOR HELP

In the unluckily event that you need to contact the emergency services during your stay, here are the numbers of the emergency services:

Police	117
Ambulance	144
Fire	118

If you can't remember the numbers, call 121. This is the central emergency number for Europe. You can call this number anywhere in Europe and they will redirect you to the nearest emergency service.

There is also a walk-in clinic at Zeughausgasse 22

9000 St. Gallen. The Arthaus St Gallen is open 365 day a year and they can treat most common aliments on the spot and give further advice if needed. The members of the staff can also speak English.

8. BORROW A FREE BIKE

Rather than walking through the city, why not speed things up and take a bike with you as you explore?

At St Gallen train station you will see signs for "Velostation" or "bike station. Follow the signs and you will find a bike station where you are able to borrow a bike for free for the day.

9. ENJOY A LOCAL TIPPLE

Appenzeller is a local liquor that is made from 42 different herbs and spices. The exact recipe of this alcoholic drink remains a secret, known only to the Ebneter family, who first developed the drink.

The drink contains no additives and is made from 100 per cent natural ingredients. It can be enjoyed neat or on the rocks but can also be added to cocktails and long drinks to give an extra punch of flavour.

10. SHOPPING IN THE SUPERMARKETS

Coop and Migros are the big players in Switzerland, even though there are lots of other foreigner competitors now entering the market.

Beware that there are difference between these two supermarket players. Migros brands itself as the family-friendly supermarket and as a result it doesn't sell alcohol or tobacco. It took me a while to realise that there wasn't any beer on the shelves there.

Apart from that, both supermarket stock a wide-range of food and other goods. This is handy to know if you are on a self-catering holiday.

11. BE KIND TO THE ENVIRONMENT

Drinking water is available through the city at the local drinking fountains so there is no need to buy expensive bottled water while you are in Switzerland.

Bring your own refillable bottle or instead of throwing your shop-bought water away simply refill it.

Many of the local supermarkets will charge you for plastic carrier bags and larger paper carrier bags. To cut down on your waste, make sure that you bring a canvas shopping bag with you or reuse carrier bags.

At many places around the city there are containers to recycle waste. Simply dispose of your waste, either paper, plastic bottles (PET), tin cans or unrecyclable waste into the bins provided.

12. SOUVENIRS TO TAKE HOME

Many people opt to buy fridge magnets, key rings, cows carved out of wooden and T-shirts with them when they go back home.

There is nothing wrong with choosing these as your lasting mementos of your time in Switzerland but I would recommend something that is more practical and durable, while still remaining quintessentially Swiss.

A Victorinox penknife is about as Swiss as you can get and comes in many different designs to choose from. Engraving services are also available if you want to make the item even more personal.

Staff in the shops are always willing to give you their expert advice and make recommendations that are personal to you.

FOOD AND DRINK

13. TAKE THE BUS TO APPENZELLER CHEESE FACTORY

You can't come to Switzerland and not sample the cheese that it is world-famous for!

The Appenzeller Cheese Factory is located in the small village of Stein and is only a short bus ride away from St Gallen. The factory has a large demonstration area where you can watch the cheese being produced before your very eyes and every Wednesday and Sunday there are tours for visitors. Unfortunately, these tours currently only take place in German.

There is also a small restaurant where you can try the products before you buy. I would recommend try the meat and cheese platter, which is delicious and big enough to share. It will almost certainly convince you to buy something to take home with you.

Smaller guests will also be entertained in the large playground area outside where they can release their energy on trampolines, slides and swings, while adults relax with a drink on the nearby picnic benches.

14. VISIT THE OLDEST BREWERY IN SWITZERLAND

There is no shortage of breweries in Switzerland. In fact, there are almost 900 breweries currently in operation – a huge amount for such a small country.

St Gallen is home to the Schützengarten, a brewery that was founded in 1779 and is still producing a wide range of award-winning beers to this day.

The museum is located on Sankt Jakob-Strasse in the Old Town. It has daily tours and an excellent exhibition which housed over 140 different Swiss beers.

15. TRY THE LOCAL SPECIALTIES

St Gallen is well-known for its Olma Bratwurst and since 2008 has been registered as Protected Geographical Indictations.

This means that only bratwurst made according to the original recipe in St Gallen is allowed to bear the name. The original recipe can be found in a Swiss cookbook dating back to the end of the 1800s.

Additionally, the food can only be made from pigs that have been reared in Switzerland and neighbouring Principality of Leichtenstein.

16. SOMETHING FOR A SWEET TOOTH

If you are a fan of sweet things, nothing could be better than finding a café and trying a Biberli. This traditional baked good can be found the length and breadth of Switzerland but originates from the St Gallen area.

The delicious tasting cake, which isn't well-known outside the borders of Switzerland, is a white almond filling encased in a gingerbread and honey dough. My mouth is salivating just thinking about it. It is a perfect accompaniment to cup of tea or coffee in the afternoon.

These snacks can also be found in local supermarkets and are a handy treat to take with you on a hike or long walk.

17. ENTER THE EXCITING WORLD OF SCHOGGILAND

The Maestrani Chocolarium is the place for chocolate lovers to unite and explore the amazing world of chocolate.

The chocolate factory is located 20 minutes from the centre of St Gallen in Flawil. There is a huge range of activities on offer: from tours to chocolate making course and events for birthdays and weddings.

There are free car parking spaces are available as well as charging bays for electric cars. You also have the possibility of buying a combined ticket to visit the Appenzeller Cheese factory and the Chocolarium and save money on the entrance fees.

18. DINE AT A LOCAL LANDMARK

The Berggasthaus Aescher-Wildkirchli is yet another stunning local landmark that is not to be missed.

The location became famous after being featured on a National Geographic cover. The Berggasthaus is built directly next to an imposing mountain.

It is only accessible via the Wasserauen-Ebenalp cable car and then you have a short walk of about fifteen minutes through the Wildkirchli caves.

The restaurant has lots of delicious offerings, including very tasty rösti that I can highly recommend.

19. EAT AT THE BEST RESTAURANT IN ST GALLEN

If you are looking for a unique culinary experience then you need to book at table at Einstein Gourmet while you are visiting St Gallen.

The restaurant has been awarded with a Michelin Star and has 17 Points Gault-Millau. Its offerings are exquisitely prepared French cuisine that are a delicious treat for your stomach and your eyes.

The ingredients used are always fresh and carefully prepared to construct unforgettable dishes.

The restaurant is located on Berneggstrasse 2, 9000 St Gallen. Advanced booking is highly recommended.

Museums and Culture

20. VISIT THE NATURAL HISTORY MUSEUM

The Natural History Museum of St Gallen moved to its new, modern location as recently as 2016 but it was first established in the 1840s.

Like every National History Museum, it houses a
huge collection of exhibits which are educational for
all the family. In addition to the fixed exhibitions,
special exhibitions are displayed on a regular basis.

A fantastic place to go if the weather is bad.

21. TAKE A TRIP TO ST GALLUS AND THE ABBEY

If you are interested in Baroque architecture the
decorative features and the exquisitely painted
ceilings of this Abbey are not to be missed. And if
you're not, it's still something that you shouldn't
miss!

The Abbey is one of the oldest and best preserved of
its kind in the world and is incredibly beautiful.

If I had one piece of advice it would be to make sure
that you arrive there early to avoid the crowds. An
early morning wake up call might not be everyone's
favourite way to start the day but being able to walk

in these surroundings in peace makes it more than worthwhile.

22. GUIDE YOURSELF ON A TEXTILE TOUR

St Gallen embroidery has been regarded as a world leader since around 1850. For this reason, the city is an amazing place for lovers of textiles and fashion to explore.

You can download the TextileStGallen App for free which gives you access to an individual city guide. Using the app you will be guided through the major points of interest for textiles in the city.

The best thing about the app is that once it has been downloaded it can be used completely offline – without needing WiFi – so that your data roaming charges are kept to a minimum.

The App will also guide you to the Textile Museum which offers tours, a large textile library and special exhibitions throughout the year.

23. APPRECIATE ART

Art lovers will love the Kunstmuseum (or "Art Museum") which is located in the city centre.

The museum holds one of the broadest collections of art in the whole of Switzerland with pieces ranging from the Middle Ages until the present day. The museum is most proud to boast of its collection of Dutch paintings and classic modern art.

You can find the museum on Museumstrasse 32, 9000 St. Gallen. Remember that the Museum is closed on Mondays but open on Sundays.

24. EXPLORE ST GALLEN CATHEDRAL AND LIBRARY

The Roman Catholic Cathedral of St Gallus and Otmar has been part of the Diocese of St Gallen since 1847.

The cathedral is heaped in history and was completed in 1767. The celebrated designer of the building is Peter Thumb, who also designed the Abbey's library.

The library is the oldest library in Switzerland and a UNSECO World Hertiage Site and boasts a collection of over 170'000 volumes. You can also see a seventh-century BCE Egyptian mummy on display that the library has owned since 1836.

The cathedral is located at Klosterhof, 9001 St Gallen.

25. GALERIE SONJA BANZIGER

One of the most highly-rated art galleries in St Gallen, this small art gallery is definitely worth a visit to see its interesting collection of pieces.

The art on display is regularly changed which keeps the exhibitions fresh and interesting.

The museum is only open during limited times so, if you want to make sure that you get to view the art, you should check the times on the website to avoid disappointment.

The address of the gallery is Magnihalden 17, 9000 St Gallen

OUTDOOR AND ADVENTURE ACTIVITIES

26. COOL OFF IN SUMMER

Summers in Switzerland can get very hot and humid. Temperatures can peak at around 35°C or 95°F during the warmer months. The higher temperatures means that lakes manage to heat up to a pleasant temperature.

Drei Weieren ("Three Ponds") is a great spot for locals and tourists alike to cool off during these warmer summer months. Located off Bitzostrasse, the three ponds are a place to relax, swim and enjoy the fresh air. You will be able to find changing facilities and warm showers powered by solar energy there as well as playgrounds for children to play and table tennis tables.

BBQing, or "grilling" as the Swiss say, is very popular during the summer and there are plenty of communal BBQ places available to use. Simply buy whatever you want from one of the supermarkets and enjoy your meals. This is a great way to meet locals as they enjoying heading down there to relax after work and enjoy the sunshine.

27. ENJOY A BAREFOOT TRAIL

When I first heard about this activity I was more than a touch sceptical. Going hiking can sometimes be tough wearing suitable footwear. The thought of hiking without shoes seemed like a strange and messy exercise to me.

It does take a while to get used to the sensation of walking through the fields and tackling obstacles without wearing socks and shoes but, after the initial uncertainty, the combination of the scenery and the new sensations makes the experience worth it.

Once I started, I was so surprised at how much fun it was. The hike itself begins in Jakobsbad and continues to Gontenbad. The route is easy and is suitable for children. It takes about 1 hour 30 minutes to complete.

At the end of the trail there are foot washing stations where you can get yourself cleaned up. There is also a whirlpool and a steam room available to use for a small fee if you need additional pampering. Make sure you remember to bring a towel and a swimming costume if you want to use these facilities.

28. ATZMÄNNIG

Atzmännig a leisure park that has a range of activities to offer throughout the year.

In summer a toboggan run is open, as well as a rope adventure park, plenty of hiking trails and rides for all of the family to enjoy.

In winter the area is transformed by the snow into a place for skiers, snowboarders and people who want to try their hand at snow-shoeing to explore.

Prices and opening times vary so make sure you check their website for the most up-to-date information.

During the winter season the streets are illuminated by 700 stars which gives the place a very Christmassy feel.

29. FIND FRIENDS ON A MOUNTAIN

887 metres above sea-level and overlooking the city is the mountain of Freudenberg, which literally means "friend mountain". This mountain provides a great outlook across the city and provides some peace and quiet away in nature.

There are many pathways up to the top but the most accessible place is from the Drei Weieren.

The pathways are clearly marked and are suitable for anyone with good mobility.

30. MAKE A TUNE ON THE TOGGENBURG TONE TRAIL

The Toggenburg Tone Trail (or "Klangweg" in German) is a themed hiking trail with interactive musical instruments spaced along the way.

On every part of the way, there are musical instruments that children can bang, clatter or knock to make noise. It's great fun and there are always surprising sounds to be made along the way.

The walk is suitable for families with strollers or prams but the whole distance is about 6km so it does take a while to complete depending on how young your little ones are.

There are picnic areas and places to grill along the way so it is a good idea to bring food with you to prepare and eat.

31. ENJOY THE THRILLS OF SÄNTISPARK

Säntispark is a leisure water park that is great fun if you want to relax or have some serious fun.

There are various slides with different degrees of fun and difficulty. If that isn't your cup of tea, there is also thermal spas, saunas, a range of gym equipment and massage treatments available.

It is open 365 days a year and had an on-site restaurant as well as excellent changing facilities.

EXPLORE THE CITY

32. GRAB A BARGAIN AT THE MARKETS

There is no better way to get to know a place and the people who live there than to head down to the market on market day. Looking through the different produce next to locals helps to give you a real sense of the place and the culture.

There is no shortage of markets in St Gallen. From May until November the farmers' market takes place on Marktplatz every Saturday.

Two additional seasonal markets are held in April and in October which last for a week. These are typically bigger than the regular farmers' market and host a fun fair.

33. CHILL OUT ON THE RED CARPET

Take some time out from sightseeing and chill out on St Gallen's very own red carpet.

The areas was commission to be redesigned in 2005 to give the quarter a new and unique identity. The area is now known as the city lounge or the red carpet of St Gallen. The total area is 4'600 square meters and is covered with red plastic granulate, which gives the place a very unique look.

There is a café and a restaurant available as well as an interesting set of sculptures, fountains and trees places throughout the quarter which makes it a relaxing place to sit and take a break.

It is very easy to find: walk along Metzgerstrasse towards the train station and stay left. It's virtually impossible to miss with its vibrant red colour.

34. VISIT THE OLD TOWN DURING WINTER

The Old Town is the most historic part of the city and is an interesting place to explore. The beautiful streets are broken up by town squares where crowds gather during the day.

In the wintertime, the streets are littered with stands and stalls selling Christmas wares and products at the annual Christmas market. You can buy anything from custom-made Christmas decorations, herbs and spices, cheese and knitwear.

35. HIKE UP THE STEPS AT ST LAURENZENKIRCHE

If you are feeling energetic and want to get a fantastic view over the whole city, hike up the 186 steps (yes, it is exactly that many, I counted them myself) up the tower of St Laurenzenkirche. Although it sounds like a lot of effort, the view at the top is definitely worth it. You can find the church just around the corner from the cathedral on Marktgasse.

The tower is only open from March until November and is only open for two hours per day. So you will need to plan ahead if you want to experience the dizzy heights. It's best to double check ahead of time via their website to see when the tower is open and avoid disappointment. Admission costs 5 CHF. From the top you can take spectacular photographs as a memento of your trip.

36. RIDE THE MÜGGLEGGBAHN

This sounds like it could be the name of a train in Harry Potter for non-wizards but it isn't.

Behind the Abbey District is a gorge called Mühleggschlucht.

The very first part of the public transport system in St Gallen was built here when the Müggleggbahn was constructed for people wanting to get up and down the gorge quickly.

The ride from top to bottom only takes 90 seconds and, if you have a public transport ticket for the local area, it is already included in the price. If not make sure you buy a ticket from one of the machine at the location. You can select English as the language on the ticket machine to make sure that you buy the right ticket.

37. STADT PARK

Known to locals as the green oasis in the city, the Stadt Park (or "city park") is a great place to enjoy the good weather.

The park is equipped with restrooms, water fountains and playgrounds.

It covers 33,737 m² and is the largest green space in the city centre. You can find it situated between the Kunstmuseum (Art Museum) and the Historisches und Völkerkundemuseum (Historical Museum and the Museum of Ethnology).

SPECIAL EVENTS

38. LOOKING FOR A UNIQUE EXPERIENCE?

The Olma Fest in St Gallen, my favourite festival in the whole of Switzerland, takes places over 10 days in October.

The festival celebrates everything that is good about the town and showcases products made in the region. Here you can try locally produced milk, cheeses, sausages and other specialties as well as get up close and personal with cows, goats and sheep.

The highlight for me is always the Säulirennen (or "piglet racing") at the end of the day. You can inspect the piglets before the race and decide which one you think will be able to out-run the others. There is even a betting kiosk so you can put your money where your mouth is and see if your piglet is the fastest.

It's a good idea to look out for special offers that combine the entrance fee and train travel online for people wanting to visit the festival.

39. CAMP AT THE OPEN AIR ST GALLEN

If music festivals are your thing, Open Air St Gallen is the place for you. Taking place every year at the end of June, the week-long festival attracts some of the current best live acts from around the world.

The event is not cheap though, especially if you want to camp out at the venue and take advantage of one of the generous hospitality packages.

Check the website well in advance for the latest offers and dates.

40. FASCHNACHT

Faschnacht is an annual event which is held in Catholic cantons to symbolise the end of the winter season. Locals will dress up in garish costumes and parade through the streets. It's a time of year when everyone is looking to enjoy themselves and to celebrate the start of spring.

The week-long event normally take part at the end of February to the beginning but the dates change each year in accordance with Lent and Easter.

If you want to witness, or even join in, these events make sure you check the dates beforehand.

NATURE

41. WANDER AROUND THE BOTANICAL GARDENS

I love taking time out to wander around botanical gardens for an afternoon. I love it even more when the admission are free and the gardens as are amazing as they are in St Gallen.

The Botanical Gardens in St Gallen houses an extensive collection of over 8'000 native and foreign plants. There is also a humid palm house, an orchid house, a house for alpine plants as well as open air displays.

As many of the plants are housed inside so this is a great activity if the weather is not so great.

The Gardens are located behind the Natural History Museum on Stephanshornstrasse and is easy to get to by local bus.

42. CHASING WATERFALLS

If the trip up or down with the Mühleggbahn (tip number 34) is too easy for you, you could decide to find the waterfall at the top of the gorge. The hike takes about 20 minutes but is very steep and is not recommended for people who have mobility problems.

43. GET CLOSE TO NATURE AT PETER & PAUL WILDLIFE PARK

There are a lot of very good wildlife parks in Switzerland and the Peter & Paul wildlife park is no exception.

The park is free to enter and is home to a wide range of native Swiss animals, such as ibex, wild boars, deer and marmots.

It is located at Kirchlistrasse 92, 9010 St. Gallen on hill which also has impressive view of the Alpstein mountain when the weather is good. The easiest way to get there is to take the 5 or 9 bus to St Gallen, Sonne and then follow the Wildpark signs.

The path starts directly behind the station for the Mühleggbahn. You should be able to see the waterfall about halfway up the footpath on your left.

44. FIND ADVENTURE AT WALTER ZOO

The Walter Zoo's website boasts that they house 900 animals from 120 different species and these animals are waiting to meet you at what is sure to be an adventure for the whole family.

Lions have recently made a return to the zoo after a short absence while the zoo facilities were updated to offer them more space to roam around in.

In addition to the animals, there are playgrounds for children, a petting zoo and camel and pony rides.

The zoo offers a Sunday brunch during certain times of the year but you need to book in advance either online or by phone to guarantee your place at the brunch table.

The zoo is open 365 days a year but times vary depending on the season.

The Walter Zoo's address is Neuchlen 200, 9200 Gossau. The journey takes about 30 minutes by train from St Gallen city centre.

DAY TRIPS AND EXCURSIONS

45. TRIP TO A BOAT TRIP ON LAKE CONSTANCE

St Gallen is very close to Lake Constance, which borders Germany.

It is possible to take a boat trip on the lake with the Swiss Bodensee Schiffahrt. The boat will take you from Rorschach or Romanshorn on the Swiss shore to the German towns of Konstanz, Friedrichshafen, Immenstaad and Meersburg.

Boats sail at regular intervals throughout the summer and there is a good selection of refreshments available to purchase on board.

46. TAKE THE VIEW OVER SIX COUNTRIES

Säntis, a mountain and local landmark, is a great destination if you want to enjoy magnificent views over six countries. You can take the cable car from Schwägalp to get to the top of the mountain that is 2502 metres above sea level.

Because of its unique location, from the top you will be able to see six countries: Switzerland, Austria, Germany, France, Leichtenstein and Italy.

At the top of the mountain, there is a restaurant with a panoramic view offering a good selection of food and drink.

There are many hiking route in this location as well, if you are feeling energetic.

47. SPEND A DAY IN LUCERNE

Lucerne is one of my favourite cities in Switzerland and is well worth a visit. It is a two-hour journey by train from St Gallen and is known for its huge choice of watch shops. This is definitely the place to come if you want to invest heavily in a Swiss watch.

Other points of interest not to miss are:

• The Lion Monument - which Mark Twain said "(is) the most mournful and moving piece of stone in the world."

• Walk along the Chapel Bridge and check out its hidden art

• Visit the Swiss Transport Museum

48. VISIT THE LARGEST CITY IN SWITZERLAND

With a population of just over 1 million, Zurich is the largest city in Switzerland and is just over an hour away from St Gallen by train.

There are so many places to explore in Zurich. It is home some of the best museums in Switzerland, including Kunsthaus Museum which is home to famous works by the likes of Monet, Manet and Van Gogh.

Zurich is also home to FIFA, the governing body of football, and the world's oldest vegetarian restaurant, Hilti, which offers a huge variety of vegetarian and vegan dishes on a buffet.

49. VISIT A LOCAL CAPITAL CITY

The nearest capital city to St Gallen is Vaduz, the capital city of the principality of Liechtenstein. It takes around an hour by car or about 75 mins by train. If you buy a travel pass during your time in Switzerland, this ticket is also valid to travel to Liechtenstein.

Leichtenstein is famous for its medieval castles and alpine landscapes. Vaduz castle overlooks the city and is the residence of the Prince of Leichtenstein's family. Unfortunately, it is not possible to visit inside of the castle.

However, I highly recommend the Postal Museum on Städtle 37, which has a great collection of stamps and the history of the postal service in Switzerland and in Leichtenstein. The museum is completely free and there are interactive exhibits as well as interesting information about how stamps used to be produced and printed and how technology has changed these processes today.

Visit the Leichtenstein Tourist Information Centre and you can get you passport stamped with an official Leichtenstein stamp. You have to pay 3 CHF for the privilege.

50. TAKE A TRIP TO RAPPERSWIL

I would highly recommend a half or full-day trip to Rapperswil. It is a small town situated on Lake Zurich and takes about one hour by train from St Gallen.

Even though the place is small, it has a great deal to offer visitors. The Rose Gardens, deer park, the Castle and Knie's Children's Zoo are all popular attractions that are entertaining for all the family.

You can also take a boat trip to take in the beauty of the lake. However, the boats due not operate during the winter months of November to March.

TOP REASONS TO BOOK THIS TRIP

Views: Nowhere has views as stunning as the Swiss Alps

Food: Chocolate, cheese and bratwurst are an amazing combination

Nature: Either in a nature park or on a hike, nature is never far away

Culture: A rich heritage of tradition that is accessible through excellent museums and exhibitions

PACKING AND PLANNING TIPS

A Week before Leaving

- Arrange for someone to take care of pets and water plants.

- Email and Print important Documents.

- Get Visa and vaccines if needed.

- Check for travel warnings.

- Stop mail and newspaper.

- Notify Credit Card companies where you are going.

- Passports and photo identification is up to date.

- Pay bills.

- Copy important items and download travel Apps.

- Start collecting small bills for tips.

- Have post office hold mail while you are away.

- Check weather for the week.

- Car inspected, oil is changed, and tires have the correct pressure.

- Check airline luggage restrictions.

- Download Apps needed for your trip.

Right Before Leaving

- Contact bank and credit cards to tell them your location.

- Clean out refrigerator.

- Empty garbage cans.

- Lock windows.

- Make sure you have the proper identification with you.

- Bring cash for tips.

- Remember travel documents.

- Lock door behind you.

- Remember wallet.

- Unplug items in house and pack chargers.

- Change your thermostat settings.

- Charge electronics, and prepare camera memory cards.

READ OTHER GREATER THAN A TOURIST BOOKS

Greater Than a Tourist- Geneva Switzerland: 50 Travel Tips from a Local by Amalia Kartika

Greater Than a Tourist- St. Croix US Birgin Islands USA: 50 Travel Tips from a Local by Tracy Birdsall

Greater Than a Tourist- San Juan Puerto Rico: 50 Travel Tips from a Local by Melissa Tait

Greater Than a Tourist – Lake George Area New York USA: 50 Travel Tips from a Local by Janine Hirschklau

Greater Than a Tourist – Monterey California United States: 50 Travel Tips from a Local by Katie Begley

Greater Than a Tourist – Chanai Crete Greece: 50 Travel Tips from a Local by Dimitra Papagrigoraki

Greater Than a Tourist – The Garden Route Western Cape Province South Africa: 50 Travel Tips from a Local by Li-Anne McGregor van Aardt

Greater Than a Tourist – Sevilla Andalusia Spain: 50 Travel Tips from a Local by Gabi Gazon

Children's Book: *Charlie the Cavalier Travels the World* by Lisa Rusczyk

63

> TOURIST

Follow us on Instagram for beautiful travel images:
http://Instagram.com/GreaterThanATourist

Follow *Greater Than a Tourist* on Amazon.

> TOURIST

At *Greater Than a Tourist*, we love to share travel tips with you. How did we do? What guidance do you have for how we can give you better advice for your next trip? Please send your feedback to GreaterThanaTourist@gmail.com as we continue to improve the series. We appreciate your constructive feedback. Thank you.

METRIC CONVERSIONS

TEMPERATURE

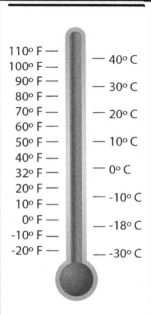

110° F —	— 40° C
100° F —	
90° F —	— 30° C
80° F —	
70° F —	— 20° C
60° F —	
50° F —	— 10° C
40° F —	
32° F —	— 0° C
20° F —	
10° F —	— -10° C
0° F —	— -18° C
-10° F —	
-20° F —	— -30° C

To convert F to C:

Subtract 32, and then multiply by 5/9 or .5555.

To Convert C to F:

Multiply by 1.8 and then add 32.

32F = 0C

LIQUID VOLUME

To Convert:..................Multiply by	
U.S. Gallons to Liters................	3.8
U.S. Liters to Gallons	26
Imperial Gallons to U.S. Gallons	1.2
Imperial Gallons to Liters.......	4.55
Liters to Imperial Gallons	22

1 Liter = .26 U.S. Gallon
1 U.S. Gallon = 3.8 Liters

DISTANCE

To convert ....Multiply by	
Inches to Centimeters	2.54
Centimeters to Inches	39
Feet to Meters......................	.3
Meters to Feet	3.28
Yards to Meters	91
Meters to Yards	1.09
Miles to Kilometers	1.61
Kilometers to Miles............	.62

1 Mile = 1.6 km
1 km = .62 Miles

WEIGHT

1 Ounce = .28 Grams
1 Pound = .4555 Kilograms
1 Gram = .04 Ounce
1 Kilogram = 2.2 Pounds

TRAVEL QUESTIONS

- Do you bring presents home to family or friends after a vacation?

- Do you get motion sick?

- Do you have a favorite billboard?

- Do you know what to do if there is a flat tire?

- Do you like a sun roof open?

- Do you like to eat in the car?

- Do you like to wear sun glasses in the car?

- Do you like toppings on your ice cream?

- Do you use public bathrooms?

- Did you bring your cell phone and does it have power?

- Do you have a form of identification with you?

- Have you ever been pulled over by a cop?

- Have you ever given money to a stranger on a road trip?

- Have you ever taken a road trip with animals?

- Have you ever went on a vacation alone?

- Have you ever run out of gas?

- If you could move to any place in the world, where would it be?

- If you could travel anywhere in the world, where would you travel?

- If you could travel in any vehicle, which one would it be?

- If you had three things to wish for from a magic genie, what would they be?

- If you have a driver's license, how many times did it take you to pass the test?

- What are you the most afraid of on vacation?

- What do you want to get away from the most when you are on vacation?

- What foods smells bad to you?

- What item do you bring on ever trip with you away from home?

- What makes you sleepy?

- What song would you love to hear on the radio when you're cruising on the highway?

- What travel job would you want the least?

- What will you miss most while you are away from home?

- What is something you always wanted to try?

- What is the best road side attraction that you ever saw?

- What is the farthest distance you ever biked?

- What is the farthest distance you ever walked?

- What is the weirdest thing you needed to buy while on vacation?

- What is your favorite candy?

- What is your favorite color car?

- What is your favorite family vacation?

- What is your favorite food?

- What is your favorite gas station drink or food?

- What is your favorite license plate design?

- What is your favorite restaurant?

- What is your favorite smell?

- What is your favorite song?

- What is your favorite sound that nature makes?

- What is your favorite thing to bring home from a vacation?

- What is your favorite vacation with friends?

- What is your favorite way to relax?

- Where is the farthest place you ever traveled in a car?

- Where is the farthest place you ever went North, South, East and West?

- Where is your favorite place in the world?

- Who is your favorite singer?

- Who taught you how to drive?

- Who will you miss the most while you are away?

- Who if the first person you will contact when you get to your destination?

- Who brought you on your first vacation?

- Who likes to travel the most in your life?

- Would you rather be hot or cold?

- Would you rather drive above, below, or at the speed limited?

- Would you rather drive on a highway or a back road?

- Would you rather go on a train or a boat?

- Would you rather go to the beach or the woods?

TRAVEL BUCKET LIST

1.

2.

3.

4.

5.

6.

7.

8.

9.

10.

NOTES

Printed in Great Britain
by Amazon

27401157R00051